know your pet

PONIES

Joan Palmer

The Bookwright Press
New York · 1989

Know Your Pet

Cats   Rabbits
Dogs   Hamsters

First published in the
United States in 1989 by
The Bookwright Press
387 Park Avenue South
New York, NY 10016

First published in 1988 by
Wayland (Publishers) Limited,
61 Western Road, Hove,
East Sussex, BN3 1JD, England.

© BLA Publishing Limited 1988

Library of Congress Cataloging-in-Publication Data

Sproule, Anna
   Ponies/Anna and Michael Sproule
      p.   cm. — (Know your pet series)
   Bibliography: p
   Includes index.
   Summary: Discusses the history of the pony and
horse, the different breeds, and their relationship to
people. Also gives instructions for feeding, housing,
grooming, and exercising a pet pony.
   ISBN 0-531-18253-3
   1. Ponies — Juvenile literature. 2. Horsemanship
— Juvenile literature. [1. Ponies. 2. Horsemanship.]
I. Sproule, Michael. II. Title. III. Series.
SF315.S67   1989
636.1'6—dc 19   88–6898
                                        CIP
                                         AC

Designed and produced by BLA Publishing
Limited, East Grinstead, Sussex, England.

A member of the Ling Kee Group
LONDON · HONG KONG · TAIPEI · SINGAPORE · NEW YORK

Photographic credits

t = top, b = bottom, l = left, r = right

cover: Trevor Hill

8, 9 Bob Langrish; 11t Bridgeman Art Library;
11b Bruce Coleman; 12 Bob Langrish; 13 Mansell
Collection; 14, 15l, 15r Trevor Hill; 17 Bob Langrish;
18t Trevor Hill; 18b Bob Langrish; 19t Trevor Hill;
20 NHPA; 21t, 21b Bob Langrish; 24 Bruce Coleman;
25 Bob Langrish; 26 Bruce Coleman; 27t, 27b, 28t,
28b, 29, 30, 31, 32, 33t Trevor Hill; 33b Bob Langrish;
34, 35, 36, 37t, 37b, 38t Trevor Hill; 38b Bob Langrish;
39 Trevor Hill; 40b, 41t Bruce Coleman; 41 Trevor
Hill; 42, 43t, 43b Bob Langrish

The Publishers would like to thank Surrey Crest
Livery for their invaluable assistance in the
preparation of this book.

Editorial planning by Jollands Editions
Illustrations by Adam Hook/Linden Artists
Printed in Italy by G. Canale & C.S.p.A. – Turin

Cover: Their smaller size, greater
mobility and responsive nature
make ponies ideal mounts for
children.

Title page: A successful relationship with
your pony can only be achieved
by gentle, thoughtful handling,
and care and attention to your
pony's health and welfare.

Contents

Note to the Reader

In this book there are some words in the text that are printed in **bold** type. This shows that the word is listed in the glossary on page 44. The glossary gives a brief explanation of words that may be new to you.

Introduction

This book is about ponies, how to understand them, how to ride them and how to care for them. You may never have a pony of your own, but some day you may get the chance to learn how to ride or to go pony **trekking**. People who love animals and the outdoor life can have a lot of fun riding ponies, so can many of those who are disabled.

What is a pony?

A pony is a small horse. As animals, ponies and horses do not differ greatly except in height. The height of a pony or a horse is measured in **hands** from a point on the back called the withers. A hand is a measurement of four inches, or about ten centimeters. The height is measured with a measuring stick, with hands and inches marked on it.

In the early part of this century, any small horse measuring less than 13 hands (h.h.) was called a pony. Today, it is usually accepted that a **breed** standing less than 14.2 h.h. is a

▲ The height of a pony or horse is measured between a point on the back called the withers and the ground. The height is given in hands. One hand is equal to four inches or about ten centimeters.

▼ These men are playing polo at Palm Beach, Florida. The horses that polo players ride are always called polo ponies, whatever their height.

pony, not a horse. But you should remember that a polo pony is always called a "pony" regardless of height, and an Arab horse is never called a pony however small it may be.

About ponies

An animal used for riding is called a **mount**. Ponies make excellent mounts for children because they are small. British ponies, like those that have lived in the wild for centuries on the moors of Dartmoor and Exmoor, are good for riding. This is because they are tough, lovable and can always be kept out on pasture, in the open. Finer-boned animals, known as **thoroughbreds**, are usually kept in stables.

Most ponies have good **temperaments**. This means they are even-tempered and not easily frightened. The Shetland pony is the smallest pony. It is very strong, but because of its size, can carry only small adults or children. The height of a Shetland pony is always given in inches rather than in hands.

▼ A pony is a small kind of horse. It does not grow into a horse as it grows older. This champion Highland pony is full-grown.

Horses and ponies through the ages

The first **ancestor** of horses and ponies lived in North America about 60 million years ago. Scientists called this early horse Eohippus, from Greek words meaning "Dawn Horse." Hardened remains, called **fossils**, of Eohippus have been discovered. These remains show that the first wild horses were the size of foxes. Later horses were about the same height as Shetland ponies.

Horses and humans

Horses were first domesticated in southern Russia some 6,000 years ago. Hunters kept them in herds near their homes and settlements to use for food. Around 3,500 B.C., a group of people called the Sumerians settled in Babylonia. They learned how to train horses and used them to draw wheeled war chariots. We know this from pictures on an ancient tablet called the Standard of Ur.

One of the oldest breeds of horse is the spotted Appaloosa. Spotted horses are known to have existed in many parts of the world.

▼ The first wild horses lived 60 million years ago, long before there were human beings. They were very small and may have looked something like the animals in the picture.

► Two hundred years ago, stage coaches drawn by a team of horses carried passengers from one city to another. The coaches stopped at inns along the road to change the horses and take on passengers. They carried ten or more people, some inside the coach and some on top.

They can be seen in Chinese paintings that are 3,000 years old. Before the horse was put to work, people had to travel overland by foot. Later, horses and horse-drawn vehicles became the most popular means of transportation until bicycles, trains and cars were invented in the nineteenth century.

Wild horses today

The Asiatic, or Mongolian, wild horse was discovered in 1881 by a Russian explorer, Professor Mikolai M. Przevalski. Przevalskis, as these horses are often called, are considered to be the oldest of all breeds of horses and ponies alive today. They are extremely rare, but there are small herds in several zoos and nature reserves.

Zebras are related to the ass and the horse. They are white with black stripes and there are three types of zebras. The Grevy's is the largest and has enormous ears.

All breeds of the domesticated ass — the donkey — have descended from the wild ass of North Africa. Donkeys vary in height and are not stupid animals as some people think. They make excellent pets, and can be ridden and driven.

▼ A few Mongolian ponies still live wild in the vast plains of Mongolia in Asia. In recent years, these ponies have become very rare.

Ponies at work

Ponies, though smaller than horses, are very strong and hardy. Their **stamina**, that is their ability to endure hardship, depends on where they were bred and the work for which they were used.

The Welsh Mountain pony, though only 12 h.h., can carry an adult and is good for trekking over rough ground. Shetland and Highland ponies, with their thick coats and sturdy limbs, can endure the cruelest weather conditions. Tough ponies like these were used to pull carts and even small buses in the factory towns of Britain.

Today, ponies are used mainly for sports and fun. Once a year, in London, England, there is a van horse parade. This first started so that traders could show off their ponies and their smart vans. Now, anyone interested in pony driving can compete alongside the gaily painted carts and vans of the past.

▼ Pony trekking is fun. These people are enjoying a vacation in the Rocky Mountains. Ponies are very surefooted. They can pick their way carefully through shallow streams and along rough mountain tracks.

▲ Pit ponies, handled by young boys, were used in coal mines during the nineteenth century to pull trucks between the coal face and the elevators. Several breeds were used, including Welsh, Fell, Dartmoor and Exmoor ponies. The pit workings and tunnels were often so low that only Shetland ponies could be used.

Pit ponies

In the nineteenth century, when the deep coal mines began to use elevators, pit ponies were used to work underground. Their task was to draw the trucks from the coal face to the elevators. Many ponies worked for so long underground in the dark that when they were brought to the surface they could no longer see. However, they were loved and well cared for by the miners. Ponies no longer work underground in coal mines.

The Pony Express

The Pony Express was started in 1860 to provide a fast mail service between Missouri and San Francisco, a distance of 3,218 km (2,000 mi). Riders rode fast horses (not ponies) in three stages, each of about 20 km (12 mi), and were allowed only two minutes at each stage to change mounts. Buffalo Bill Cody was one of the most famous Pony Express riders. The Pony Express lasted for only eighteen months, but it won a lasting place in American history.

Understanding ponies

Ponies and horses have learned to trust their human friends over thousands of years. Since they are **vegetarians**, feeding mainly on grass, they have no need to kill other animals. For this reason, they are not **aggressive**, except when defending the herd, and are at heart very gentle creatures.

When ponies and horses show bad temper, it is usually because something has frightened them. Even the wild Mustang of North and South America became a useful saddle horse once it had been tamed and trained. The word "bronco," from the Spanish word meaning rough and rude, was used to describe the wildest Mustangs. Bronco-busters were the people who tamed them and broke them in.

Ponies and their senses

To get the best out of ponies, we need to understand their body language and how they behave. The **instincts** of ponies stem from their origins in the wild. The constant need was to look out for danger, and to run away or **bolt** from it.

Hearing, vision and sense of smell are all well developed in a pony. With its large head, a pony can detect sounds and movements better than most animals. The large, mobile ears, and the eyes placed on each side of the head help the pony to take in messages from every direction.

For this reason, you should always approach a pony from the front so that you do not startle it. Hold out your hand and speak gently to it. When you are near enough, pat or stroke its lower neck or shoulder. Never make sudden, jerky movements and always speak to a pony before handling it.

▼ You should approach a pony very gently from the front and talk to it as you do so. It may want to sniff your hand, but keep your hand still with fingers together and the palm flat.

Body language

A pony, of course, cannot talk but it can show its mood by various movements of the body. We call this body language. A raised head with ears pricked forward means that the animal is interested or suspicious. If a pony is miserable, it hangs its head. When a pony puts its ears back and shows the whites of its eyes, it is angry.

However, when a donkey lays its ears back, this means that it is pleased. Also, seeing the white of the eye in an Appaloosa does not mean temper. The Appaloosa eye looks like the human eye as there is white on the eyeball surrounding the colored part.

▼ ▶ **The pony on the left has its ears pricked forward. This means that it is interested and alert. But the other pony has ears that are laid back, meaning that it is nervous or displeased.**

How we describe ponies

It is important to learn the names given to the various parts of a pony's body. You can get this information from the picture on this page. These parts are known as the **points** of the animal. We also use this word "points" to indicate the mane, the tail and the lower part of the leg when describing the color of a pony.

▶ When you see a group of ponies or horses like the one in the picture, you realize how they all differ in appearance. The best way to describe each pony is by its color and markings.

Points of a pony

Color

The main colors of ponies are black, brown, bay and chestnut. A white horse or pony is called a "gray." The bay color varies a lot. A bay is a brown colored horse with black points. A brown horse or pony is dark brown, or nearly black in color, with brown points.

▲ The different parts of a pony's body are known as the points. Some of these are shown in the picture above. On page 17 you can see the head markings, called stripe, blaze and star.

stripe

blaze

star

The word Palomino, referring to the "Golden Horse of the West," is not a breed but a color type. Palomino coloring comes in various shades of gold, with a chalk white mane and tail. The name comes from Juan de Palomino who is said to have received one of these beautiful horses, known in Spain as Isabellas, from the explorer Cortes.

Markings

A piebald horse or pony is one that shows large patches of black and white. A skewbald animal shows large patches of white and any other color except black.

In the United States, piebalds and skewbalds are also known as "Paints" and "Pintos." The word Pinto comes from a Spanish word meaning painted.

Pony breeds — British Isles

In some countries, children have to learn to ride on large horses. But in the British Isles there are nine distinct breeds of pony. Very young children can learn to ride these small mounts. The British breeds have their origins in mountains and moorlands, and are hardy and surefooted. They are ideal for beginners and for pony trekking in groups.

The Shetland

This breed has existed for many years in the Shetland Islands of Scotland. One of its tasks was to cart seaweed for use on the land. The Shetland is an ideal first pony because of its size, only about 10 h.h. Many people keep these lovable little ponies just as pets. In color, they are mostly bay, black and brown, but there are also piebalds and skewbalds. Shetland ponies are very strong, and friendly, and they live to a good age.

The Highland

This pony is the largest of the mountain and moorland group. As it is very strong, surefooted and **docile**, it is ideal for pony trekking. The smallest Highland stands at 12.2 h.h. and the largest is about 14.2 h.h.

▲ The Shetland pony is so small that it can only carry a very young child. Shetlands are very strong and sturdy. Some children find them rather wide between their knees and therefore difficult to ride.

◄ The Highland pony is very strong and has quite a large body. This beautiful animal was judged champion at a recent Highland Show.

▼ Compare this Welsh Mountain pony with the Highland on page 18. It appears to be much less stocky and rather more graceful. Some people think that the Welsh Mountain pony is the most beautiful of all nine breeds of pony that come from the British Isles.

The Welsh Mountain

This breed has lived wild in the mountains of Wales for possibly thousands of years. Although only 12 h.h., the Welsh Mountain can carry an adult with ease. It has a friendly temperament and is very popular as a child's pony. The head and tail are often set high, which gives this pony a gay and proud appearance.

Of all the nine British pony breeds, the Welsh Mountain is thought by some to be the most beautiful. It should not be confused with the Welsh Pony (13.2 h.h.), and the Welsh Cob (14 to 15 h.h.), both of which were once bred from the Welsh Mountain pony.

The Connemara

The Connemara is a breed with a long history. Bred in western Eire, these ponies show signs of Spanish and Arab blood. The Connemara is usually gray and stands at 13 to 14 h.h. It is strong and a good jumper, but it is best as a mount for older children.

The ponies of England

There are five world-famous breeds of pony that are native to different parts of England. Some of these breeds still live in the wild as they have done for centuries. These English breeds are popular all over the world.

New Forest

Herds of these ponies still roam the New Forest in Hampshire, the woodland and heathland of their origin. They are able to survive on poor grassland and are very hardy. New Forest ponies are mostly larger than other native breeds, which makes them a good choice for teenagers.

▲ These are New Forest ponies. They are a lovely sight as they roam over their natural territory. This group includes two young foals, one gray and one black. Many people who live in the New Forest have grazing rights on the common land for their ponies. People called verderers are appointed to protect the rights of the owners.

Dartmoor

The Dartmoor pony is hardy and handsome and has great charm. It was once used for work around the tin mines of Devon and Cornwall. Today, it is the ideal all-around pony for children, and is often used by children competing in **gymkhanas**. The Dartmoor stands no more than 12.2 h.h. and is usually bay or brown in color.

Exmoor

This pony has its home in Exmoor on the borders of Devon and Somerset. The oldest of the British breeds, the Exmoor may date back to the Stone Age. Later it was possibly used as a chariot pony.

It is hardy, long-lived and affectionate, which makes it a safe mount for children. The Exmoor is much the same height as the Dartmoor, but its coat differs from other native breeds. The Exmoor coat is springy, harsh and rather dull in winter months. But some say that it shines like brass in the summer.

Dale and Fell ponies

In the north of England there is a range of hills called the Pennine Chain. The Fell pony came from the west of this range and the Dale from the east. The ponies were once used to carry lead from the mines to the ports.

The Dale is about half a hand taller than the Fell and is stockier. Of the two, the Fell pony is thought to be the best for riding.

▲ Dartmoor ponies are ideal for pony trekking. This photograph shows a party of people trekking over the moorland, which is the natural home of the Dartmoor pony.

▶ Balmoral Bramble is a champion Fell pony owned by H.M. Queen Elizabeth II. Fell ponies are powerfully built, tough and very hardy. They have plenty of hair on mane and tail.

Ponies of Asia and Europe

There are many interesting breeds of pony that originated in Asia and Europe. Some of these have long been used for work in harsh weather conditions over hard and uneven country. They are very hardy and surefooted.

The Spiti is a typical example. This sturdy, tireless little hill pony (12 h.h.) is used on the mountainsides of the Himalayas in northern India. The Spiti is gray and has short legs and hard round feet.

The Mongolian

Bred and used by the Mongolian people, this pony is also extremely hardy. Many Mongolian ponies find their way to China where they are used for sports and racing. The Mongolian is a little pony, only 12.2 to 13 h.h., with rugged strength of body and limb. This pony could not be called a beauty, and it is known to have a willful and stubborn temperament.

The Batak

This Asiatic breed, which stands about 12 h.h., is sometimes called the Deli. It is bred in the Batak hills of Sumatra and exported to other countries in large numbers. The Batak is a

▲ The Mongolian pony has a heavy head and strong shoulders. Its legs and feet are also extremely sturdy. These ponies were once used as pack animals by the Mongolian people.

▼ The Spiti is a hard working little pony. It is tough and very surefooted. It works in the foothills of the Himalayas for the people who live there and thrives only on high ground.

▼ The Batak pony has an attractive head and a high "crest" to the neck. This feature is due to Arab blood in the breed.

► The Icelandic pony is short and stocky. It has a heavy forelock and mane, and the tail is very long. Icelandic ponies are docile and friendly.

▲ The Haflinger has coloring that is very similar to that of the Palomino. This Austrian pony carries its head close to the ground when climbing hills and mountains.

▲ The Fjord pony is very stocky, and it is docile and hardworking. The chief feature of this Norwegian pony is its splendid creamy coloring.

handsome pony with a proud head and high, crested neck due to Arab blood in its past. Arabians are among the oldest and most beautiful of horses. Their influence on other breeds has been greater than that of any other horse.

The Haflinger

The Haflinger, an Austrian mountain pony, is small but sturdy. It is often used as a pack pony and for forest work because it is so surefooted. This breed first came from the village of Hafling in Austria, but Haflingers are now reared at Piber in Austria. This town is also famous for the rearing of the dancing Lipizzaner **stallions** of Vienna. Haflingers are usually chestnut in color with a flaxen mane.

The Fjord

This Norwegian pony is of ancient origin and is a hard worker. You can easily recognize the Fjord by its dun coloring with a dark stripe along the back. The mane is clipped so as to stand upright. It has a docile temperament and in some ways is similar to the Highland.

Ponies of North and South America

Today, most of the ponies found in England, Europe and Asia are also found in the New World, and all breeds have registries in the United States to record bloodlines.

The horses that were native to North and South America thousands of years ago died out, but the Spanish brought in horses and ponies once more in the sixteenth century.

The Criollo

The Criollo is the cow-pony of Argentina. This hardy pony came from Spain long ago with the explorer Cortes. The Criollo comes in many colors, including skewbald.

Another cattle-herder was the Mustang, the original "cow-pony" of the American West. However the Mustang is not really a pony, but a small hardy horse, descended, like the Criollo, from horses brought in by the Spaniards. With its wild nature, the Mustangs, or bronco, is still a challenge to riders.

▼ Mustangs are very hardy, and are full of fire and courage. But they are wild and difficult to ride. Mustangs are seldom more than 14 h.h., and are to be seen in every color. A herd of these animals is a wonderful sight.

The Pony of the Americas

This is a new breed of pony in the United States. It is a breed that has been crossed with Arab, Quarter horse and Appaloosa blood. The American Quarter horse and Appaloosa are used for many purposes and are well known for their good temperaments.

The Pony of the Americas, with this careful **crossbreeding**, has become very popular in the United States. The height for this breed lies between 11.2 and 13.2 h.h., so young American riders now have a pony of their own.

▶ Falabellas are not really ponies at all. They are miniature horses, and are the result of crossing very small thoroughbreds with Shetland ponies.

Falabella

The Falabella is in fact not a pony at all but a miniature horse. It is only 7.2 h.h. in height, and was bred by mating very small horses with Shetland ponies. This animal is far too small to be ridden, and its only use is as a pet. Falabellas may be any color.

These little animals take their name from Señor Falabella, the man who first developed the breed in Argentina. They are friendly, hardy and intelligent. It is possible to see some of these little horses at Kilveston Park in Norfolk, England, where there is a collection of South American animals.

Feeding ponies

Ponies in the wild are always on the move in search of food. Most of the day and night is spent in grazing. They survive by feeding on grass and are total vegetarians, or **herbivores**. Ponies have small stomachs, nature intending that they should have a little food in the stomach all the time, but never a lot at any time.

Out on pasture

In harsh climates, only tough native breeds of pony can live out on pasture all year round. Those people who can keep a pony on pasture need the use of a field or paddock that is well fenced. A shelter placed in a corner of the field is a good idea. Ponies do not mind rain, but they do need to be protected from cold winds.

Ponies should never be allowed to go short of water. A drinking trough should be provided and kept filled. Care must be taken that the water does not freeze in the winter.

▶ **It is best to feed a pony using a hay net like the one in the picture. If the hay is scattered loose on the ground it will get dirty and the pony may get an upset stomach.**

▼ **Ponies on pasture get their water from a field trough when they want it. The owner must check each day that there is plenty of clean water in the trough.**

Feeding for work

Ponies that have to work and are stabled cannot forage for themselves. They therefore need regular supplies of hay. They may also require grain like corn or oats for extra energy. These contain all the **vitamins** and **minerals** they need. They may also be given bran and carrots. If a pony is not working, do not feed it oats because oats makes it hyperactive, and therefore difficult for small children to handle.

The more work a pony does, the more food it needs. A pony kept on pasture and doing no work at all gets all the food it needs from the pasture during the summer months. During the winter, when there are no longer any nutrients in the grass, or if it is put to work, a pony will need hay and perhaps grain.

The food that ponies eat is not cheap to buy. Stabled ponies are usually fed twice daily, although four feeds a day is better. Having a pony involves a lot of expense and hard work.

▼ Besides eating up to three nets of hay a day, a stabled pony will also need other foods such as grain. This pony is eager for its food.

Making a start

The cost of feeding a pony is so high that only the lucky few can afford to have one. But many young people can learn to ride at a nearby stable, or can offer to help with the ponies there. If you find ponies and horses really interesting, you will soon become an enthusiast. Sooner or later you will want to learn how to ride.

Many disabled children, who cannot easily get around, gain a great deal of pleasure from riding quiet ponies. There are organizations whose members enjoy helping these children learn how to ride.

Where to learn riding

There may be a choice of several stables and instructors in your neighborhood. Visit a number of them with an adult who knows something about riding. The instructor you choose should be friendly and the stable should have good horses or ponies.

▲ Most stables have a large building where beginners can have their first lessons indoors. This is where you will learn how to mount and dismount, how to ride at the walk and the trot. The pupils follow each other around the ring and the instructor stands in the center and gives advice.

◄ Riding helps some young people who are partly disabled. It gives them enjoyment and exercise in the open air. They are helped with their riding by people who belong to organizations that help disabled children learn to ride.

It is best if there is an indoor arena where instruction can be given in all weather. There should also be plenty of land nearby where you can go trail riding. Some instructors do not take beginners away from the school area. Others take them along quiet roads and tracks, using a leading rein to control their pupil's pony.

Getting ready

Watch a lesson in progress and see what the riders are wearing. Some riders will be wearing **jodhpurs** and turtle-necked sweaters. Others may be wearing jackets and jodhpur boots too, if they are lucky. Most riding instructors are happy for children to wear jeans and comfortable, sturdy shoes or rubber boots. But everyone who rides, including beginners, should always wear a hard riding helmet for reasons of safety.

If you ride a lot, you may someday want to wear the correct riding clothes. You can usually buy these secondhand. You will find riding clothes offered for sale on the stable bulletin board, or in notices in horse magazines and local newspapers.

▼ As can be seen in this picture, young riders can wear a variety of clothing. Every rider must wear a safety helmet to protect the head from injury. The helmet must fit securely in case the rider falls or strikes an overhanging branch while riding near trees.

Saddle and bridle

Before you have your first ride it is useful to learn something about saddles and bridles. This riding equipment is usually called **tack**. Saddles and bridles make it possible for you to ride a pony and make it obey you. They are kept in a **tack room**.

The saddle

The saddle pad is placed on the pony's back for the comfort of the mount. Saddles were first used in the times when the Barbarian horsemen were attacking the foot soldiers of the Roman Empire.

Pad saddles, sometimes used on donkeys and very small ponies, are made of felt, whereas most saddles are made of leather. There are different types of English saddles for hunting and jumping, but the general-purpose English saddle is the one used for beginners.

▼ All beginners have to learn how to saddle a pony. The girth is adjusted first, then the leathers, which carry the stirrup irons.

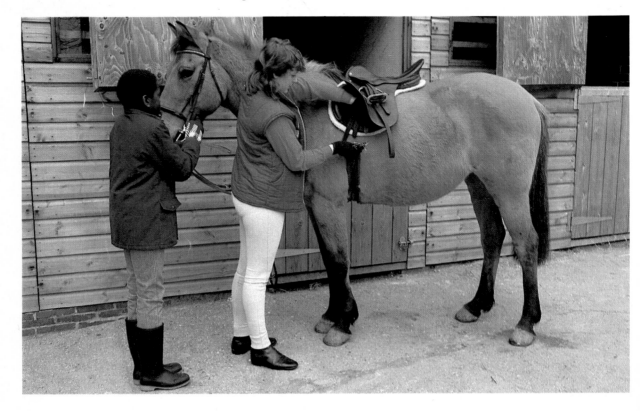

snaffle bit

▶ **Putting on the bridle is quite easy once you have been shown how to do it. It helps to talk gently to the pony at the same time. This is a good way of making friends with the pony and getting it to trust you.**

A girth, which is a band made of leather, webbing or nylon, is attached to buckles under the saddle flap. The girth is tightened up so that it fits firmly and comfortably on the pony's back. Straps known as leathers are also attached to the saddle to carry the stirrup irons. At your first lessons you will find the girth, leathers and irons in position, but you must learn to remove these when you are told to do so.

The bridle

The bridle was invented in Ancient Greece about 2,000 years ago. There are several types of bridles, but the best kind for beginners is the snaffle. This has a single bit for the pony's mouth and one pair of reins. You make the pony do what you want by the way you move your body and handle the reins. The reins are connected to the bit in the pony's mouth, so you have to handle them as gently as possible.

When you sit back in the saddle and gently draw back the reins the pony will slow down. When you lean forward in the saddle and loosen the reins slightly, the pony will quicken its pace.

Learning to ride

Over two thousand years ago there was a great soldier called Xenophon who lived in Ancient Greece. He was also a writer and a good horseman. He wrote the first books on riding skills and the stabling of horses. The rules and ideas that he gave in those books still hold true today.

However, you cannot learn to ride just by reading books. You have to listen carefully to everything your instructor tells you. Then you must try to do exactly what you are told.

► Rising to the trot, or posting, takes some time to learn. The rider rises in the saddle to one hoof beat, misses the next hoof beat, down again, and so on. The up and down movement has to be timed to the pony's hoof beats for a smooth ride.

◄ In mounting a pony, the rider starts by placing the left foot in the stirrup iron. Then the rider swings the right leg over the saddle, while holding the reins and the front of the saddle. A beginner is sometimes helped by being given a "leg-up" by the instructor.

The paces of a pony

First you will have to learn how to mount and **dismount**, how to put your feet in the stirrups and how to sit squarely in the deepest part of the saddle. Once you have mastered this you will begin to learn the various **paces** of the pony. These are the walk, the trot, the canter and the gallop. You will only learn the gallop when you have really mastered riding.

To start with, you will be taught to ride the pony at walking pace. You sit deep in the saddle with your back straight, your knees tight against the saddle and your heels well down. The next stage, the trot, may take

▼ The Spanish Riding School in Vienna, which has existed for over 250 years, uses Lipizzaner stallions. Riders are taught to reach perfection in horsemanship. They have to learn movements such as the Levade, shown in this picture.

longer to master. It is a "two-beat" pace, with the rider "posting," or rising up in the saddle and down again. Next time you hear a pony clip-clopping along the road, imagine yourself rising slightly in the saddle on the "clip," and sitting down again on the "clop."

The canter is a movement in three beats. It is a more natural pace for the pony, with one pair of fore and hind legs in front of the other pair. You have to learn to sit well down in the saddle and not bounce up and down. The gallop is a movement in four beats, with each foot striking the ground separately. It is very exciting, but that comes later!

A good seat

A skilled rider is described as having a good seat. You will develop a good seat once you have learned to sit correctly at the various paces. You also have to think all the time how the pony is going to move, and to grip with your knees so as not to lose balance in the saddle. Then you will be a good rider!

Grooming

Learning to groom a pony is very important, and it is hard work. Someone has to do the grooming and it should be the person who has the pleasure of riding. In any case, it is a good way of getting to know the pony you ride.

If a pony does not live in the wild, its skin and feet will suffer unless it is carefully groomed each day. Grooming is not just a matter of improving a pony's appearance, like cleaning a car. It also helps to prevent disease by keeping the skin clean.

Grooming routines

A pony that is kept on pasture does not need as much grooming as a stabled pony. In the skin there are natural oils. These pick up the dust so that the grease and the dust together make the coat waterproof and keep the pony warm. Donkeys, in particular, often have their own favorite dust patches that they like to roll in.

curry comb

sponge

mane comb

▼ **This girl is using a body brush to groom the pony. In her other hand she is holding a curry comb for cleaning the body brush.**

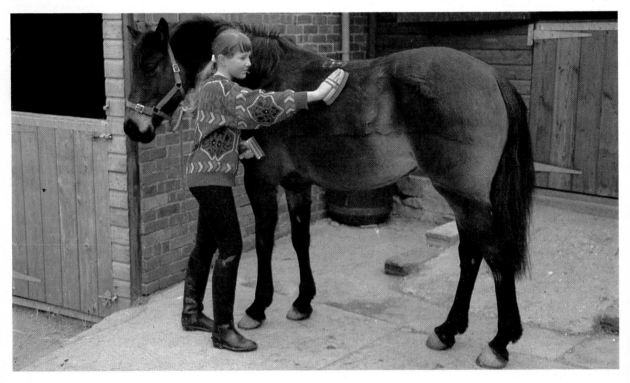

► The long hair that flows from the top of a pony's neck is the mane. This has to be combed out often with the use of a mane comb.

▼ You will have to learn to recognize the different pieces of grooming equipment. They are illustrated here and their uses are described in the text.

hoof pick

dandy brush

water brush

body brush

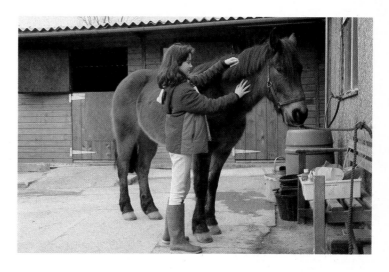

However, this does not mean that a pony or donkey kept on pasture should be neglected. It should be inspected each day and brushed or combed, and the eyes and **muzzle** carefully sponged. The feet should also be picked out with the hoof pick. At the end of the summer, ponies and horses grow a thick coat in preparation for the winter. The thick coat becomes a disadvantage when working. The pony may then sweat too much, and dry off so slowly that it becomes chilled.

In the stable

The stabled pony should be brushed off and have the feet picked out before work. After work, the pony needs to have a thorough grooming and this may take a long time. In the evening, when the pony's day blankets are replaced by night ones, it has to be brushed yet again. The equipment can be seen in the illustrations. The body brush is for general use and to remove dust. This brush can be cleaned from time to time with the curry comb. The dandy brush has stiff bristles and is used mainly for removing dried mud. The water brush is used damp on mane and tail.

35

Stable management

There is a lot of work when ponies are stabled. The bedding must be dealt with; grooming, feeding (little but often) and watering have to be done throughout the day. Then there is blanketing at the end of the day, and cleaning the tack, the stall and the stables. These things are all part of good stable **management**. In racing stables, grooms do the work. At most riding schools, the children are expected to help.

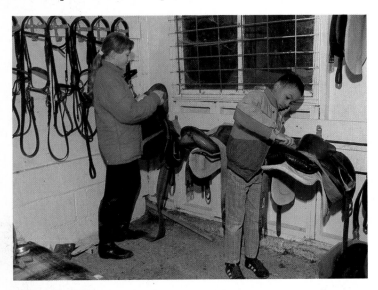

◄ In the tack room you can see bridles hanging neatly on the left, and saddles on the right. Everyone helps to keep the tack clean and polished. It is all part of learning about ponies.

The pony's bedding

Most ponies have straw for bedding. It makes a comfortable bed and, as it is bought in bundles known as **bales**, it is easy to store. Make sure that you can tell the difference between hay, which is dried grass, and straw, which is the stalks of wheat. Barley straw is used in stables also. It is not a good idea to use oat straw. The pony may eat it and get a stomachache.

Wood shavings, sawdust and peat moss are also sometimes used as bedding for ponies, but straw is mostly used since it is cheaper to buy and easier to get rid of.

► This pony has been groomed and is now waiting in the stable yard while its stall is being mucked out. There are metal rings fixed to the wall at various points around the yard. The pony is tethered to the ring by means of a lead rope attached to the bridle.

Mucking out

The daily job of cleaning out the stable is usually called mucking out. The pony's droppings and dirty straw are forked into a wheelbarrow and removed to the manure heap. Then some fresh straw is put into the stable. For this job, a pitch fork, a shovel, a wheelbarrow and a plastic bucket are needed.

Some people who keep ponies just cover the dirty bedding with fresh straw and only muck out once a week instead of each day. This way of doing things is known as **deep littering**. It is better to muck out each day if there is time to do so.

It is important to fork out all the bedding and hose down the stable from time to time. When the bedding is remade, the straw has to be raised around the sides of the stable. This prevents the pony from harming itself on the stone or wooden walls if it kicks out or rolls.

▲ Mucking out is very hard work, and everyone helps. The stall has to be swept out after all the muck has been removed.

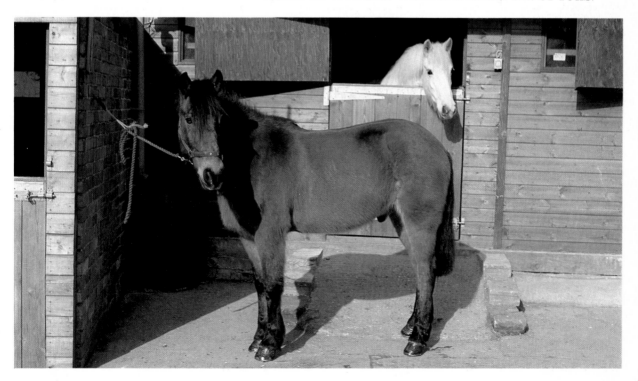

Exercise and health

A pony kept on pasture and not working will develop a big stomach, known as a hay belly. It will be unable to canter or gallop without sweating and feeling uncomfortable. This is known as being in soft condition. A stabled pony that has been carefully fed and exercised is said to be in hard condition.

It takes about six weeks to bring a pony that has been out on pasture into hard condition. During this time it is first taken out at a walk every day, and then walking and trotting until it has hardened up. As the exercise increases, the amount of grain in the feed is also increased.

Shoeing

Unlike a pony that runs wild, a pony used for riding has to be shod at regular intervals. If this is not done, the wall of the foot, which is rather like a fingernail, will wear away. Shoeing prevents the pony's feet from wearing down. There are two methods of shoeing. Hot shoeing is when the shoe is shaped on a forge to fit the foot and nailed on hot. With cold shoeing, a ready-made shoe is adjusted and nailed on cold. Shoeing is carried out by a **farrier** and does not hurt the pony.

▲ When a pony needs to have new shoes fitted the farrier is called in. Ready-made shoes are nailed into place without hurting the pony at all.

◄ When a horse or pony has to be taken a long distance, a motor horse box is used. There is always a danger of the animal kicking against the side of the box while traveling. The pony's legs are bandaged to protect it from injury.

Ailments and injuries

Because a pony is unable to vomit as humans can, a stomachache, known as colic, can be very serious. Colic can be caused by sudden changes of diet or by drinking dirty water. There are other illnesses, such as influenza or coughing. All of these ailments have to be dealt with by a vet.

Ponies and horses at work can be very easily injured if care is not taken by the rider. Many injuries are caused as a result of thoughtless handling and poor horsemanship. A badly fitting saddle or girth can cause sores on the pony's body. These will become infected if they are not properly treated.

Hard or thoughtless riding can often result in sprains or injuries to the pony's legs. Once you start learning to ride, spare a thought for the pony. A good understanding between you and the pony will always be rewarded.

▲ Racehorses have to be schooled and kept in the peak of fitness by expert trainers. This picture shows schooling taking place on the Lambourn Downs in England.

Breeding ponies

A male horse or pony used for breeding is called a stallion and should be over four years old. The female is called a **mare** when she has reached the age of four. When we say that a pony is well-bred it means that its parents and ancestors have also been well-bred. The breeder, who has expert knowledge and skill, will match the good points of a mare and a stallion. If their ancestry is good, and they have no weak points, the result of the mating is likely to be a first-class offspring. The offspring is called a **foal**.

Successful breeding calls for a lot of skill on the part of the breeder. It can also prove expensive since the owner of the stallion will charge a **stud fee** for the stallion's services. Stallions are not usually turned out to graze with mares. Because of this, the stallion sometimes leads a rather lonely life.

◀ When a foal is first born it looks weak and helpless. At this time, the mare and her foal should be left on their own and the foal should not be handled.

The mare and her foal

A mare takes about 340 days to foal from the time of mating. Once the vet has confirmed that the mare is in foal, her diet is increased. The mare's hoofs have to be watched carefully because of the extra weight she will be carrying as the foal grows inside her body.

Very soon after the birth the foal is able to stand up on its spindly legs. Then it begins to follow its mother about and learn from her. There are few finer sights than the mare and her foal. The foal will feed on its mother's milk for five or six months and can be handled quite young by the owner. This creates trust, which is valuable when the time comes for schooling and training.

The young pony

From the age of one to four years, a male foal is called a **colt**, and a female is called a **filly**. The young pony must be cared for and fed for three or four years before it can be used for riding. Because of this, only the lucky few can afford to breed a pony and feed it until it is old enough to be ridden.

▲ Two or three days after it is born a foal will be standing. It soon starts to skip about on its spindly legs. The owner can now gently handle or carry the foal, holding it around the chest but without touching head or neck.

▼ The first step in training a pony to jump is to "lunge" it over a pole laid flat on the ground as shown in the picture.

Gymkhanas and horse shows

Once you have learned how to ride you may decide to become a member of the Pony Club. This organization has local clubs in countries all over the world. Its aim is to encourage young people to ride well. Every year teams from all branches compete in an exciting competition. It is for well-trained ponies but they do not have to be of the highest quality.

In England, the six winning teams take part in the Mounted Games Championships. This takes place at the Horse of the Year Show at Wembley, near London.

Pony competitions

The Pony Club games in which riders take part are similar to those that are included in gymkhana events around the country every summer. They include a sack race. In this, each member of the team has to ride to the center line, jump off, get into a sack, and lead his or her pony to the other end. There, another team member is waiting to take over the sack.

▼ Each year in England, children take part in the Mounted Games at the Horse of the Year Show at Wembley, London. After stepping over the pots, each child has to mount again and race to the finish. There are many other fun competitions and team races.

▲ In this event, judging is taking place for the Green Hunter at Palm Beach, Florida. When a horse or pony has not completed its training, it is said to be "green."

▼ There are Pony Club events throughout the world. Here, in Bangkok, a young rider is being judged for jumping skills.

At local horse shows and gymkhanas, young riders can take part in various classes. An "in-hand" class is one in which the pony is led on a show lead. Other classes might be an in-hand class for Palomino ponies, and a ridden class for mountain and moorland ponies. There might also be a class for the best-turned-out pony and rider.

Horse shows and events

Today most people can watch pony and horse riding events on television. You can watch international horse shows, show jumping and horse trials — without leaving your home.

Riding is now a sport in which many nations of the world can take part. The Pan American Games are held every four years for the nations of North and South America. The Olympic Games also take place every four years. Any nation of the world can enter a team of riders if it wishes to do so. Knowing about ponies and horses, you will probably take an interest in all these events, even if you are only a beginner at riding.

Glossary

aggressive: always ready to quarrel or attack

ancestor: an animal living a long time ago from which a present day animal has descended

bale: a bundle of hay or straw packed up tight so that it can be easily handled or stored

bolt: to run away out of control when frightened

breed: a kind or class of pony having parents of the same kind. Each breed of pony can be recognized by its size, shape, color, etc.

colt: a male foal under four years old

crossbreeding: breeding a pony or horse from a male of one pure breed and a female of another pure breed

deep littering: putting fresh bedding on top of old bedding and manure. This is usually done to save time

dismount: to get off a pony or horse

docile: ready to learn and easy to handle

farrier: a person who attends to the hoofs and feet of ponies and horses

filly: a female foal under four years old

foal: a male or female offspring of a pony or horse

fossil: the hardened remains of a living thing that died millions of years ago

gymkhana: a pony or horse show with games

hand: the unit used for measuring the height of ponies and horses. One hand is equal to four inches or about ten centimeters. If a pony is ten hands high, it is written 10 h.h.

herbivore: an animal that eats vegetable food only

instinct: natural behavior that does not have to be learned

jodhpurs: riding breeches with a tight leg-covering that goes down to the ankle

management: controlling something and making it work well

mare: a female pony or horse able to breed

minerals: natural materials, such as iron, that are found in the ground and are needed in small amounts in a pony's food

mount: (1) a pony or horse used for riding. (2) to get on a pony or horse

muzzle: the jaws and nose of a pony or horse

paces: the leg movements of a pony or horse. The four paces are the walk, the trot, the canter and the gallop

points: (1) the parts of the body and the names given to those parts. (2) the tips of the ears, the mane, the tail and the ends of the legs nearest to the ground

stallion: a male pony or horse able to breed

stamina: the bodily strength and ability to endure

stud fee: a fee paid to the owner of a stallion chosen to breed with a mare

tack: the saddles and bridles used for ponies and horses. The word is short for tackle

tack room: the room where saddles and bridles are kept

temperament: the nature of a pony or a horse, and its temper, which may be good, even or bad

thoroughbred: of pure breeding

trekking: riding in a group over a long distance at a fairly slow pace

vegetarian: an animal that lives only on vegetable food

verderer: a person appointed to look after the rights of those using common land for grazing their ponies, as in the New Forest, Hampshire, England

vitamins: substances found in small amounts in food; vitamins are needed for good health

Further reading

America's Horses and Ponies by Irene Brady. Houghton Mifflin, 1976
Closer Look at Horses by Joyce Pope. Gloucester Press, 1987
Horses and Foals by Fern G. Brown. Franklin Watts, 1986
Horses and Riding by Georgie Henschel. Warwick Press, 1986
Wonders of Ponies by Sigmund Lavine. Dodd, Mead & Co., 1980

Useful addresses

American Humane Association, 5351 South Roslyn Street, Englewood, Colorado 80111
American Society for the Prevention of Cruelty to Animals, 441 East 92nd Street,
New York, New York 10028

Index